The National Gallery

BOOK *of* SAINTS

The National Gallery

BOOK *of* SAINTS

NATIONAL GALLERY PUBLICATIONS
LONDON

Saint Paul

Saint Paul Writing (detail)
Pier Francesco Sacchi, EARLY 16TH CENTURY

Paul, originally called Saul, was an early persecutor of Christians but was dramatically converted on the road to Damascus by a vision of Christ. As a result he became a tireless preacher, travelling all over the Mediterranean. His three principal journeys were to Cyprus, Asia Minor and eastern Greece, and Ephesus, Macedonia and Achaia. Nero ordered him to be beheaded in Rome in about AD 66.

Although Paul is traditionally portrayed holding a sword and a book, he is here writing, in Greek, a passage from his first letter to the Corinthians: 'Charity suffereth long, and is kind; charity envieth not; charity vaunteth not itself, is not puffed up.' Sacchi was active in the late fifteenth and early sixteenth century, in Genoa. Paul shares his main feast day with Peter on 29 June, but 25 January celebrates his conversion.

January

1	2	3	4
5	6	7	8
9	10	11	12
13	14	15	16

Saint Sebastian

The Virgin and Child with Saints Francis and Sebastian (detail)
Carlo Crivelli, 1491

Sebastian was a soldier in the Roman army during the third century. He was secretly a Christian and helped confessors in prison. He was made a captain of the praetorian guard by Diocletian, but when the emperor discovered his faith he ordered Sebastian to be shot to death by arrows. Sebastian survived this, however, and challenged Diocletian for his cruelty; for this he was clubbed to death. As bubonic plague was often likened to God's arrows, Sebastian became one of the saints invoked against this disease. His story greatly appealed to artists of the Renaissance, as it provided an opportunity to depict a young male nude in a religious context. Sebastian's feast day is 20 January.

Crivelli was born in Venice and was active in the region of the Italian Marches in the second half of the fifteenth century. He was very successful as a maker of altarpieces such as this one, which was painted for a church at Fabriano.

January

17	18	19	20
21	22	23	24
25	26	27	28
29	30	31	

SAINT MATTHEW

Saints Matthew, Catherine of Alexandria and John the Evangelist (detail)
Stephan Lochner, *c*.1445

Matthew was a Jewish tax collector before he became an apostle and evangelist. He was the author of the first Gospel, and was martyred in either Ethiopia or Persia. As an apostle he is depicted with the sword or axe of his martyrdom or the money bag of his early profession; here he is shown writing his Gospel; an angel, his symbol as an evangelist, is by his side. His feast day is 21 September.

Lochner was the leading painter in Cologne in the mid-fifteenth century. In this altarpiece panel the bright colours are softly modelled in great detail, and the gold background is punched with a rich design. The painting was presented to the Gallery by Queen Victoria in 1863.

FEBRUARY

1	2	3	4
5	6	7	8
9	10	11	12
13	14	15	16

Saint Dorothy

Saints Peter and Dorothy (detail)
The Master of the Saint Bartholomew Altarpiece, *c.*1505-10

The legend of the virgin martyr Dorothy relates that on the way to her execution, ordered by Diocletian, she was jeered by a lawyer, Theophilus, for refusing to marry or to worship idols. He taunted her by asking her to send him fruit from the garden of Paradise. Dorothy agreed and prayed for this at her death. An angel appeared to Theophilus with a basket of three apples and three roses; the lawyer converted and was himself martyred. Dorothy's feast day is 6 February.

The Master of the Saint Bartholomew Altarpiece was a German painter, active from about 1470 to 1510. He lived in Cologne, but his work shows a strong Netherlandish influence. This late painting formed the left wing of an altarpiece, and was presented to the Gallery by Queen Victoria.

February

17	18	19	20
21	22	23	24
25	26	27	28

29

SAINT FRANCIS

The Stigmatisation of Saint Francis (detail)
Sassetta, 1437-44

Francis of Assisi (1181-1226) was the son of a wealthy cloth merchant, who renounced his inheritance in response to a call from Christ to restore his church, and began a new life as a mendicant preacher. He attracted others committed to the same ideals and they lived a communal life of Christian orthodoxy and poverty. In 1212 Francis went to the Holy Land, to convert the Saracens and denounce the Crusaders for their loose living. He impressed, but did not convert, the Sultan himself.

This panel from an altarpiece painted for the church of St Francis in Borgo Sansepolcro, Tuscany, is by Sassetta, one of the leading Sienese painters of the fifteenth century. It shows Saint Francis receiving the Impression of the Stigmata, or Five Wounds of Christ, on Mount La Verna in 1224. Francis was canonised in 1228. His feast day is 4 October.

MARCH

1	2	3	4
5	6	7	8
9	10	11	12
13	14	15	16

Saint Anne and Saint Joachim

Charlemagne, and the Meeting of Saints Joachim and Anne at the Golden Gate (detail)
The Master of Moulins, *c.* 1500

Anne and Joachim were the parents of the Virgin Mary. Neither is mentioned in the Scriptures, and no historical details of them are known. Anne is first mentioned by name as the Virgin's mother in the apocryphal Gospel of James, written in the second century. Here the two are shown embracing outside the walls of Jerusalem at the Golden Gate. It was at this meeting that the Virgin was said to have been miraculously conceived. The feast day of both saints is 26 July.

The Master of Moulins takes his name from a triptych in Moulins cathedral in France, which he made for the Bourbon court. This painting is part of the left-hand side of an altarpiece; the right-hand side, depicting the *Annunciation,* is in Chicago.

MARCH

17	18	19	20
21	22	23	24
25	26	27	28
29	30	31	

Saint Mark

Saint Mark (?) (detail)
Cima da Conegliano, *c.*1500

Mark the evangelist is probably the John Mark whose mother's house in Jerusalem was a meeting place for the apostles. He travelled with Peter and Paul, and his Gospel, probably written in Italy, is said to record the teachings and memoirs of Peter. He was sent by Peter to Egypt, where he became Bishop of Alexandria. He was martyred under Nero in about AD 74. In the ninth century his body was taken to Venice, whose patron saint he became. His evangelical symbol, the lion, is everywhere evident in that city. Mark's feast day is 25 April.

Cima da Conegliano was one of the most prolific artists in Venice at the end of the fifteenth century, and he may have been trained by Bellini. The identification of Saint Mark here is not certain, but likely; a companion panel shows Saint Sebastian.

April

2	3	4
6	7	8
10	11	12
13	14	15	16

Saint George

George was probably a soldier, martyred in about AD 303 in Palestine. According to his legend a terrible dragon terrorised the land, demanding one sacrifice each day. When this fate fell on the king's daughter she went to her death dressed as a bride. George speared the dragon and led it captive with the princess's girdle. He told the king and people he would kill it if they would turn to Christ; 15,000 were subsequently baptised. As the embodiment of the ideals of Christian chivalry, George was a fitting saint to be adopted as patron of England, and other countries, in the Middle Ages. His feast day is 23 April.

This is a rare completed oil painting by Moreau (1826-98), a leading French Symbolist painter. The design is influenced by Raphael, and the style by Delacroix.

April

17	18	19	20
21	22	23	24
25	26	27	28
29	30		

SAINT JOHN THE EVANGELIST

The Virgin and Child with Saints and Donors (detail)
Hans Memlinc, *c.*1475

John, James and Peter were all sons of Zebedee, and as apostles were privileged to witness such events as Christ's Transfiguration. John was entrusted by Christ on the Cross to adopt Mary as his own mother. He was persecuted under Domitian but escaped with Mary to Ephesus, where he died an old man. His Gospel stresses the divinity of Christ and the importance of Charity, and his symbol as an evangelist is the eagle.

This painting forms the right-hand panel of a triptych by Memlinc, a German painter whose style was formed in the Netherlands and was influenced by van der Weyden and Bouts. The altarpiece was made for Sir John Donne, in Bruges, and honours his two name saints. Saint John's main feast day is 27 December; 6 May commemorates his escape from martyrdom under Domitian.

MAY

1	2	3	4
5	6	7	8
9	10	11	12
13	14	15	16

Saint Lucy

Saint Lucy (detail)
Carlo Crivelli, 1476

Lucy was a virgin martyr who died in about AD 304 under Diocletian. Her story, like many others, was fictitious but powerful. A rich Sicilian, she renounced her wealth and was betrayed to the authorities by her suitor. The judge ordered her to be violated in a brothel, but she was made miraculously immovable. An attempt to kill her by burning also failed and she was finally killed by the sword. She holds her eyes on a dish, as she reputedly gave these to a pagan admirer.

The panel is part of an altarpiece painted for the church of St Dominic in Ascoli Piceno. It was once thought to have formed part of the 'Demidoff Altarpiece', the high altarpiece Crivelli made for the same church. Saint Lucy's feast day, 13 December, falls on the shortest day of the year in Sweden and is celebrated in a festival of light.

May

17	18	19	20
21	22	23	24
25	26	27	28
29	30	31	

Saint John the Baptist

The Virgin and Child with the Magdalen and Saint John the Baptist (detail)
Andrea Mantegna, 1490s

John's mother, Elizabeth, a cousin of the Virgin Mary, was told by an angel that despite her advanced years she would bear a son, who would prepare the way for the Messiah. John baptised Christ and later lived the life of a hermit in the desert. He was imprisoned for denouncing the incestuous union of Herod and Herodias. Herodias' daughter, Salome, one day so pleased Herod by her dancing that he promised her anything she desired. Prompted by her mother, Salome demanded the head of John the Baptist on a plate, and Herod granted her wish. John's feast day is 24 June.

The scroll around the Baptist's cross in Mantegna's beautiful altarpiece is inscribed with the words he used to describe Christ: 'Behold the Lamb of God who taketh away the sins of the world.' Mantegna, court artist in Mantua, achieved a renown unparalleled among living artists in the fifteenth century.

June

1	2	3	4
5	6	7	8
9	10	11	12
13	14	15	16

SAINT PETER

Saints Peter and Paul (detail)
Attributed to Carlo Crivelli, PROBABLY 1470S

Simon and his brother Andrew were fishermen on the Sea of Galilee, and apostles of Christ. Christ gave Simon the name Peter, meaning rock, as he was the rock on which the Church would be built and the keeper of the keys to the kingdom of heaven. Peter worked the first miracle after Christ's death, and became the most notable miracle worker. Traditionally he is said to have been persecuted under Nero and crucified upside down in about AD 64. Peter is most often portrayed with keys, as here, or with fish, to symbolise his profession. His feast day is 29 June.

This panel was part of a polyptych painted by Crivelli for a church in Porto San Giorgio, in the Italian Marches.

JUNE

17	18	19	20
21	22	23	24
25	26	27	28
29	30		

Saint Mary Magdalene

The Virgin and Child with the Magdalen and Saint John the Baptist (detail)
Andrea Mantegna, 1490s

Mary Magdalene is generally identified with the penitent sinner who anointed Christ's feet in the house of Simon. It was Mary Magdalene who went to the sepulchre to anoint the body of Christ and to whom the risen Christ appeared on Easter Sunday morning. In later life she is said to have travelled to France, where she preached to the people of Provence and died at St Maximin. She is the patron saint of repentant sinners and of the contemplative life, and her feast day falls on 22 July.

Mary Magdalene is usually depicted holding a pot of ointment, as in this altarpiece by Andrea Mantegna, who was the court artist at the Gonzaga court in Mantua from 1459 to 1506. It is not known for which church the painting was made, but it was certainly a late work.

July

1	2	3	4
5	6	7	8
9	10	11	12
13	14	15	16

Saint Margaret

Saint Margaret (detail)
Francisco de Zurbarán, 1630-34

As the daughter of a pagan priest in Antioch, Margaret was disowned when she became a Christian, and lived as a shepherdess. According to legend she was tortured by the governor of Antioch for refusing to marry him and was swallowed by a dragon, who burst open to release her. For this reason she is venerated as the patron saint of childbirth. She continued to preach the Christian message, and was ultimately beheaded by Diocletian. She is often portrayed as a shepherdess with a dragon, as in this painting by Zurbarán, where she holds a crook and a Spanish saddlebag. Margaret's feast day is 20 July.

Zurbarán was the leading artist of Seville in the 1630s. Some of his work shows a marked Italian influence, particularly from Caravaggio.

July

17	18	19	20
21	22	23	24
25	26	27	28
29	30	31	

Saint Dominic

Saint Dominic (detail)
Workshop of Giovanni Bellini, *c*.1515

Dominic Guzman (*c*.1170-1221) grew up in Spain and in 1201 became prior of the Austin community of Osma cathedral. In 1204 on his way to Denmark he met some Albigensian heretics and resolved to devote his life to converting them to the Truth. For this he trained men and women who formed communities devoted to study, teaching and prayer. He was a good organiser and his missionary communities spread all over Western Europe. He died in Bologna and was canonised in 1234. His feast day is 8 August.

Bellini, who died in 1516 after a career of over 50 years, was one of the most influential Venetian artists of his time. This late painting from his workshop shows his pioneering portrayal of light. The sitter was probably Brother Teodoro, a Dominican from Urbino.

August

	2	3	4
	6	7	8
	10	11	12
3	14	15	16

Saint Helena

The Vision of Saint Helena (detail)
Paolo Veronese, c.1560-65

Helena (c.250-330) is thought by some sources to have been British. She was the mother of the first Christian Roman Emperor, Constantine, who honoured her greatly. Her husband, however, had divorced her when he became emperor. Helena was converted to Christianity late in life, and was said to have had divine guidance in her quest for the exact location of the True Cross, on which Christ was crucified. In Veronese's painting Helena receives this inspiration in a dream. She died on a pilgrimage to the Holy Land and was buried in Rome. Her feast day is 18 August.

Veronese, named after his birthplace Verona, moved in the 1550s to Venice where he became one of the leading painters of the late sixteenth century. This painting shows his sophisticated use of luminous colour.

August

17	18	19	20
21	22	23	24
25	26	27	28
29	30	31	

Saint Michael

The Virgin and Child; Saint Michael; Saint Raphael (detail)
Pietro Perugino, 1496-1500

In the Book of Revelation the Archangel Michael is the principal fighter of the heavenly battle against the devil. His cult began in the East, where he was invoked for the care of the sick, and spread to the West. In the tenth century a Benedictine abbey was founded at Mont-St-Michel in Normandy to commemorate an earlier apparition of the saint there. He is depicted either slaying a dragon (the devil) as here, or weighing souls as part of the Last Judgement. Michael's feast day is 29 September.

Perugino, who died in 1523, was active mainly in Perugia. He was praised in his lifetime for the sweetness of his work, which is evident in this altarpiece panel. He greatly influenced Raphael, who was probably his pupil.

September

1	2	3	4
5	6	7	8
9	10	11	12
13	14	15	16

Saint Jerome

Saint Jerome in his Study (detail)
Vincenzo Catena, *c.*1510

Jerome was a fourth-century monk and a Doctor of the Church. He is most famous for producing the first standard Latin text of the Bible, known as the Vulgate version. He dreamed that God condemned him for being a scholar of Classics rather than of Scripture, and subsequently lived as a hermit in the Syrian desert for five years, learning Hebrew. At the end of his life he went to Bethlehem, where he set up a monastery. Although the office of cardinal did not exist in Jerome's day, he is sometimes shown with a cardinal's wide-brimmed hat, as here. His feast day is 30 September.

Catena was a Venetian painter who in 1506 seems to have been an associate of Giorgione. This painting shows his careful observation of light and his feeling for quiet compositional harmony.

September

17	18	19	20
21	22	23	24
25	26	27	28
29	30		

Saint Ursula

Saint Ursula (detail)
Antonio de Solario, 1514

The story of the virgin martyr Ursula and her companions has no basis in history, and became increasingly elaborate over the centuries. She was said to have been the daughter of a Christian British king, who betrothed her to a pagan prince. She asked for three years' delay before her marriage, during which time she and ten companions sailed away in ships with a thousand companions each. They sailed to Cologne, where they were all finally martyred by the Huns, whose chief Ursula refused to marry. The citizens of Cologne buried them and built a church in their honour. Ursula's feast day is 21 October.

Solario was active in northern Italy in the early sixteenth century. This painting is the side panel of an altarpiece made for Paul Withypoll, a merchant taylor.

October

1	2	3	4
5	6	7	8
9	10	11	12
13	14	15	16

Saint Luke

Saint Luke painting the Virgin and Child (detail)
Follower of Quinten Massys, *c.*1520(?)

Luke was a Greek physician, one of the apostles and a disciple of Paul whom he accompanied on some of his missionary journeys. He is the author of the third Gospel, where he tells some of the most moving parables, such as those of the Good Samaritan and the Prodigal Son. Luke's artistry with words may be the basis of the tradition that he was a painter who made icons of the Virgin Mary, which is what he is doing here. He is the patron saint of artists and physicians, and his feast day is 18 October.

This painting was probably the inside shutter of an altarpiece. It is by a follower of Quinten Massys, who was the leading painter in Antwerp from about 1466 to 1530.

October

17	18	19	20
21	22	23	24
25	26	27	28
29	30	31	

Saint Catherine

Saint Catherine of Alexandria (detail)
Raphael, *c.*1507

According to legend Catherine was a fourth-century Alexandrian princess who was persecuted for her Christianity and for refusing to marry the emperor. She disputed successfully with fifty philosophers called in to dissuade her of her beliefs, and was then tortured on a wheel, which miraculously broke. She was finally beheaded and her body transported to the top of Mount Sinai. She is thought of as the 'bride of Christ' because in a vision she was given a ring by the Infant Christ. She was a popular subject for artists, being frequently depicted, as here, with her wheel. Catherine's feast day is 25 November.

Raphael painted this panel in Florence shortly before leaving for Rome. The graceful figure of the saint turns enraptured towards a heavenly light.

November

1	2	3	4
5	6	7	8
9	10	11	12
13	14	15	16

SAINT CECILIA

Saint Cecilia (detail)
Roman School, 17TH CENTURY

The Roman-born Cecilia was a third-century Christian noblewoman who refused to consummate her marriage to the pagan Valerian, who then himself converted and was martyred. Cecilia converted her persecutors, but at a trial was sentenced to be suffocated in her bathroom. This failed, and at her beheading she took three days to die. The tradition that made Cecilia the patron saint of music is thought to come from the story that at her wedding the organs played and she sang in her heart to God, that she might remain pure. When the Roman Academy of Music was founded in 1584 Cecilia was made its patron. Her usual emblem, an organ, is included here but she is also depicted with other musical instruments, such as a lute. Her feast day is 22 November.

NOVEMBER

17	18	19	20
21	22	23	24
25	26	27	28
29	30		

SAINT NICHOLAS

The Madonna and Child with Saint John the Baptist and Saint Nicholas of Bari
(The Ansidei Madonna) (detail)
Raphael, 1505

Nicholas was Bishop of Myra in Lycia, south-west Turkey, in the fourth century. The number three dominates his legend: he gave three bags of gold to three girls for their marriage dowries to save them from prostitution, raised from the dead three boys, rescued three drowning sailors and saved from death three unjustly condemned men. The first of these acts is the origin of his link with pawnbrokers and the three golden balls of their sign. The cult of Santa Claus derives from his patronage of children and the custom in the Netherlands of giving them presents on his feast day, 6 December.

Raphael painted this altarpiece for the Ansidei family chapel in San Fiorenzo, Perugia. Although it is dated 1505 it was probably begun in 1504, before Raphael's visit to Florence.

DECEMBER

1	2	3	4
5	6	7	8
9	10	11	12
13	14	15	16

Saint Stephen

The Virgin and Child with Saints ('The Demidoff Altarpiece') (detail)
Carlo Crivelli, 1476

All we know of Stephen's life comes from the Acts of the Apostles in the Bible, which says he was one of seven deacons appointed by the apostles to oversee the distribution of alms to the faithful and to help with preaching. He was an eloquent preacher and a great scholar. He was also the first Christian martyr: in about AD 35 he was stoned to death for blasphemy. The persecutor Saul, who later converted and was known as Paul, was present and consented to his death. Saint Stephen is the patron saint of deacons, and was invoked against headaches. In this panel by the northern Italian painter Crivelli, he is depicted with three stones, the symbols of his martyrdom, and a book of the Gospels. His feast day is 26 December.

December

17	18	19	20
21	22	23	24
25	26	27	28
29	30	31	

SAINTS' FEAST DAYS

JANUARY

20 Saint Sebastian
21 Saint Agnes
25 Saint Paul

FEBRUARY

5 Saint Agatha
6 Saint Dorothy
24 Saint Matthias

MARCH

1 Saint David
17 Saint Patrick
19 Saint Joseph

APRIL

4 Saint Ambrose
23 Saint George
25 Saint Mark
29 Saint Peter Martyr

MAY

19 Saint Dunstan
30 Saint Hubert

JUNE

11 Saint Barnabas
24 Saint John the
   Baptist
29 Saint Peter &
   Saint Paul

JULY

3 Saint Thomas
15 Saint Swithin
20 Saint Margaret
22 Saint Mary
   Magdalene
26 Saint Anne &
   Saint Joachim
29 Saint Martha

AUGUST

8 Saint Dominic
18 Saint Helena
24 Saint Bartholomew
28 Saint Augustine

SEPTEMBER

21 Saint Matthew
26 Saint Cosmas &
   Saint Damian
29 Saint Michael
30 Saint Jerome

OCTOBER

4 Saint Francis
18 Saint Luke
21 Saint Ursula

NOVEMBER

1 All Saints
22 Saint Cecilia
23 Saint Clement
25 Saint Catherine
   of Alexandria
30 Saint Andrew

DECEMBER

4 Saint Barbara
6 Saint Nicholas
13 Saint Lucy
26 Saint Stephen
27 Saint John the
   Evangelist

List of Works

Saint Dominic
Workshop of Giovanni Bellini
ACTIVE *c.*1460; DIED 1516
Canvas, 63.9 x 49.5 cm.

Saint Jerome in his Study
Vincenzo Catena ACTIVE 1506-1531
Canvas, 75.9 x 98.4 cm.

Saint Mark (?)
Cima da Conegliano 1459/60- *c.*1517/18
Panel, 103.2 x 40.6 cm.

*The Virgin and Child with Saints Francis
and Sebastian*
Carlo Crivelli 1430s- *c.*1494
Panel, 175.3 x 151.1 cm.

*The Virgin and Child with Saints
('The Demidoff Altarpiece')*
Carlo Crivelli 1430s- *c.*1494
Panel, 61 x 40 cm.

Saint Lucy
Carlo Crivelli 1430s- *c.*1494
Panel, 91 x 26 cm.

Saints Peter and Paul
Attributed to Carlo Crivelli
1430s- *c.*1494
Panel, 93.3 x 47 cm.

Seven Saints
Filippo Lippi *c.*1406-1469
Panel, rounded top, 67.9 x 151.8 cm.

*Saints Matthew, Catherine of Alexandria
and John the Evangelist*
Stephan Lochner
ACTIVE 1442; DIED 1451
Panel, 68.6 x 58.1 cm.

*The Virgin and Child with the Magdalen and
Saint John the Baptist*
Andrea Mantegna *c.*1430/31-1506
Canvas, 139.1 x 116.8 cm.

Saint Luke painting the Virgin and Child
Follower of Quinten Massys
EARLY 16TH CENTURY
Panel, 114 x 35 cm.

*Charlemagne, and the Meeting of Saints Joachim
and Anne at the Golden Gate*
The Master of Moulins
ACTIVE 1483 OR EARLIER TO *c.*1500
Panel, 71.8 x 59.1 cm.

Saints Peter and Dorothy
The Master of the Saint Bartholomew
Altarpiece
ACTIVE *c.*1470- *c.*1510
Panel, 125.7 x 71.1 cm.

The Virgin and Child with Saints and Donors
Hans Memlinc
ACTIVE 1465; DIED 1494
Panel, wings 71.1 x 30.5 cm.

Saint George and the Dragon
Gustave Moreau 1826-1898
Canvas, 141 x 96.5 cm.

The Virgin and Child; Saint Michael;
Saint Raphael
Pietro Perugino LIVING 1469; DIED 1523
Panel, 127 x 60 cm.

The Madonna and Child with Saint John the
Baptist and Saint Nicholas of Bari
(The Ansidei Madonna)
Raphael 1483-1520
Panel, 209.6 x 148.6 cm.

Saint Catherine of Alexandria
Raphael 1483-1520
Panel, 71.5 x 55.7 cm.

Saint Cecilia
Roman School, 17TH CENTURY
Canvas, 143.5 x 108.9 cm.

Saint Paul Writing
Pier Francesco Sacchi c.1485-1528
Panel, 106 x 81.9 cm.

The Stigmatisation of Saint Francis
Sassetta 1392(?)-1450
Panel, 87.6 x 52.7 cm.

Saint Ursula
Antonio de Solario
ACTIVE 1502-1518 (?)
Panel, 84 x 40 cm.

The Vision of Saint Helena
Paolo Veronese 1528(?)-1588
Canvas, 197.5 x 115.6 cm.

Saint Margaret
Francisco de Zurbarán 1598-1664
Canvas, 163 x 105 cm.

Front cover illustration
Saint Catherine of Alexandria (detail)
Raphael, *c.* 1507

Back cover illustration
Saint Michael
Piero della Francesca, 1469

Title page illustration
Seven Saints
Filippo Lippi, *c.*1406-1469

© National Gallery Publications Limited 1994
5/6 Pall Mall East, London SW1Y 5BA

Devised and written by Robyn Ayers

Printed in Italy by Imago
NGPL Stock Number 301026
ISBN 1 85709 072 1